ANOTHER SPRING

A light hearted poetic and successful journey through adventures, trials and challenges as a research patient from diagnosis and the shock of the unknown to a fit and stable regime - over sixteen years later. To hopefully bring insight with diary, treatment, results and photographs of coast, countryside and flowers recorded along the way. Managing medication. The positive effects of exercise. The influence of diet with health and well being and to hopefully promote knowledge and awareness of Myeloma and hope for a cure and to gratefully acknowledge the endless kindness, care and generosity received along the way from dedicated members of the research teams, my husband, family and friends.

Special thanks to
Darren Hendley & Mortons Media Group
for their generosity and help with publishing
'Another Spring'

A garden full of promise, purple crocus peeping through.

FOREWORD

What a priviledge to introduce this extraordinary book written by a very brave and talented country woman.

It tells of frustrations, hopes and emotions but chiefly celebrates success.

Mavis is a gifted writer of prose and photographer of people and life.

The book is a faithful record of her health including pioneering research and treatment.

A delightful and entertaining book.

R. Bentley Nelstrop FRAgS

ST PAUL'S FROM THE SOUTH BANK
Surging down the River Thames you could feel we were in the heart of a great world metropolis

CONTENTS *(and some favourite photographs taken along the way)*

2007   (Revlimid Clinical Trial began 7 November 2007)

In Pursuit of Excellence ....page 10

'The Promise' & **Treatment Dates** ....page 12

A Fragile Link *(November 2007* ....page 14

The Pills *(November 2007)* ....page 18

2008   (Complete Remission confirmed November 2008 *[see appendix iii])*

An Age of Miracles *(January 2008)* ....page 20

Remission, Hope, Optimism, Happiness *(April - July 2008)* ....page 22

The Future *(July 2008)* ....page 26

The Glow of Autumn *(October 2008)* ....page 27

2009

With Luck *(January 2009)* ....page 28

A Good Mile *(2008 – 2009)* ....page 30

Daybreak *(September 2009)* ....page 32

Firelight *(November 2009)* ....page 33

2010

A Special Kind of Gift ....page 34

Endless Snow *(March 2010)* ....page 36

2011   (Revlimid Treatment began 31 January 2011 *[see appendix iv])*

Overdrive! *(February 2011)* ....page 38

Revlimid – Seven months on *(August 2011)* ....page 39

Eighth Month and Down to 15mg ....page 40

Oh What a Treat to Garden Again *(November 2011)* ....page 42

2012

Kick on *(February 2012)* ....page 43

Take Time...page 44

Endless Care *(The whole story!)* ....page 46

The Simple Basics...page 48

Don't Stand About *(March 2012)* ....page 51

Warts and All PP5!! *(March 2012)* ....page 52

A Marathon to Success *(March'12)* ....page 54

Back on Track *(April 2012)* ....page 56

Days Without End *(August 2012)* ....page 58

High Summer...page 60

2013

!!MOVING!! **STABLE** ....page 61

Evening flight *(August 2013)* ....page 62

SUNRISE - Thorntree Cottage *(November 2013)* ....page 64

2014

Those few precious minutes (March 2014) ....page 65

Antibiotics on standby ....page 66

Mud on your Boots! *(September 2014)* ....page 68

'Whatever Next' - Steroids! ....page 74

2015

Current Results and Medication *(Treatment Session 60 -* **STABLE***)*...............page 76

Over the Tide *(September 2015)* ....page 78

THE HEALING POWER OF A DIARY ....page 80

2016

Appendix

The Promise of Spring..*i*

About **MYELOMA - DEFINITION** *(contact details for* **MYELOMA UK** *and* **MAGGIE'S***)*..........*ii*

REVLIMID CLINICAL TRIAL *(began 7 November 2007)* ....*iii*

REVLIMID and DEXAMETHAZONE TREATMENT *(began 31 January 2011)*...........................*iv*

2003 to 2019 ....*page100*

'Quotes and Sayings' collected for inspiration

PHOTOGRAPHS

1. Cover 'A good Mile'

3. Early purple Crocus

5. St Paul's

11. Lesser Tortoiseshell butterfly on Teazle

13. Primroses beneath a shady hedge

17. Across the sea to Ireland

19. Sunflower

23. Mountain stream

24. Fritillaries

29. Daffodils at home in the snow

31. Norfolk terriers

35. Paper White rose from Sarah

37. Call Ducks playing in the snow

41. Thistle – watercolour

45. Swans at Pasture Lane

49. Frosty yellow rosebud

53. Pink Perfection

55. Teazle – watercolour

57. Overlooking Wells harbour

59. Burnham Overy Staithe

63. Harvest time

67. Wildlife at Glandford ford

69. Sparkling sea to Scolt Head

71. Early. Tide out. From coastal path

73. Flood line

75. Turnstones

77. Towards Brancaster from Scolt Head

79. Over the tide

81. Sunset

83. Snowdrops in January

95. Salthouse beach

97. Bluebell woods

99. A fragrant drive

100. Victoria Plum blossam

Cover 'Thank you' watercolour - Elisabeth

Diary   Photographs   Poems

PROGRESS
of a
MYELOMA RESEARCH PATIENT
REVLIMID CLINICAL TRIAL
King's College, London

begins 7 November 2007

Revlimid Treatment
City Hospital, Nottingham

begins 31 January 2011

Mavis Mary Knott

IN PURSUIT OF EXCELLENCE

'DIFFERENCE IN THE DETAIL'

Simple facts

First the shock of diagnosis, then the initial impact of treatment, I suffered intensely with ignorance at first. You do not know what is happening to you. It is so hard to get it right. Who can you turn to for help? It is the bits of 'know how' that make such a difference. The generous tips handed out along the way. Simple, positive, effective knowledge, lack of it is so deeply frustrating. You don't know how to deal with the impact of medication when you feel rough. You wonder what happened to common sense. Ignorance is so painful. But knowledge aids success, gives confidence, helps recovery and assists carers to be positive, helpful, understand and communicate. It allows you to do your very best to get maximum results with treatment. The learning curve is vertical when first diagnosed. You so want to get it right. Lack of knowledge is complete frustration. The Myeloma helpline and information booklets were a lifeline when being hit hard by treatment. So many people have been quite wonderful with a great outlook. Information is available on line. But it takes time to collate 'know how' through experience. Have endeavoured to put a little into verse.

Diagnosis and treatment may now be decided on a laptop. Technology has moved on. Research, results and treatment have advanced, a miracle of modern science. But success requires knowledge to quietly apply the detail in the pursuit of excellence.

LESSER TORTOISESHELL BUTTERFLY ON TEAZLE
The sun beats down, the garden stirs and dances in the fragrent air

THE PROMISE

I promised I'd record the way
That medication hit's the days
I must admit its pretty tough
Light headed, weak and short of puff
Lets hope the research finds remission
And soon Myeloma's in submission!
Don't even drive those first two weeks
Rest, walk, hot baths and lots of sleep
Then wake up trembling with the dawn
A cup of tea and its soon gone
So free from stress and rest and fight
Good books and music in the night
The timings right, the battle's on
Just get stuck in until its gone
Lots of fluid, lots of prunes
Fruit and veg its over soon
Photos, painting, magazines
Results are good it's like a dream
Then off again another go
But paraprotein's getting low!

January 2008

Diagnosis Lincoln County	*February 2003*
Stem Cell Transplant Nottingham	*October 2004*
Velcade Trial Nottingham	*September 2006*
Revlimid Trial Kings, London	*November 2007*
Complete Remission	
Revlimid Treatment Nottingham	*January 2011*
Revlimid Treatment stopped	*April 2018*

13

A FRAGILE LINK

Having spent the day on turbo-charge, steroids do focus the mind with great energy, I could have spring cleaned and run the Marathon! I wrote 'The Pills' as a plea for effective information at handover. Just a simple sheet in the pack would be so valued - how to take medication effectively whilst protecting the patient. Diet ideas and contact numbers. It would be an enormous help and comfort to the Patient and the family at a very crucial time when they so want to get it right.

After the 'build up' knowing the proteins are rising. Then being considered for treatment. Preparation (bloods - bone marrow - skeletal survey - ECG - interview) The crucial day arrives when the treatment prescription is handed over.

It took from August when I knew proteins were beginning to rise to November 2007, to be fortunate enough to begin the Revlimid Trial.

Perhaps I should have had some foresight to ask for information. We did not have Internet connection it could possibly have been easily downloaded. It is nearly five years since my first effective chemotherapy treatment by tablets. So the response to steroids was a known experience.

Research, training, time, knowledge and vocation come together - a whole industry - when medication is handed to the Patient. The Patient is handed a bag of the unknown. They can't spell them let alone pronounce them. They are a foreign language. They are frightening and you are desperate to get it right.

I wrote them all down and then tried to work it out - there were 40 tablets that first day - got it wrong and then asked for help. A fact sheet in the bag of prescription and research drugs would have been a godsend.

I tried to think of everything in positive preparation to get results. Just getting treatment (turned down by the PCT) was so fortunate. We thought there were no Revlimid Trials in Britain but David got on his laptop and my Consultant said she would have a word with a colleague she would see at a meeting. To my amazement she rang with the vital number - it was the same day the PCT turned me down.

We were going to Ireland and my husband wanted to cancel the holiday. But thanks to modern technology Judith arranged the appointment as we picnicked in wonderful light by an Irish Sea loch down on the Dingle peninsular.

Then there were the logistics of getting there, we took a bank loan to cover expenses and the travelling, but landing at Dublin North Wall with our caravan and tackling the M50 ring road were good preparation. Even train times and connection details were received. We couldn't find Denmark Hill on the London map at the back of the Road Atlas - still haven't found it on the map!

Sarah and I cased the route and the times that first day. Found the hospital - from the wrong station. A friendly porter said the hospital could be accessed from either station. After a good walk and the wrong entrance we got ourselves sorted thanks to another excellent map, but it took a second visit to know which way we were going up the long corridor!

So it was quite a logistical exercise to even arrive at Clinic. Of course, I would love to have started treatment on the same day! Had blood test results from Nottingham two days previously and those taken at my GP's the week before (so Nottingham would have results when I went to Clinic!). You will do everything that might effect a good result. It is your Life.........and I am loving it.........

Who would have thought. Travelling to London again, in touch, with family for company. That alone is a wonderful bonus. We have fun. Time to catch up from start to finish. We live busy lives and the luxury of a day together when business and family usually have first call is precious.

We boarded the overland Thames Link train from Kings Cross to Black Friars Bridge. We picnicked looking down the Thames to Tower Bridge. The view is glorious and the starlings love the crumbs and the sun has been shining over London for us. Then onto the train for Denmark Hill with a great London Pub just outside the station. It is lovely to sit outside in the sunshine and enjoy a fresh orange juice and then it is only five minutes walk to Kings.

It is an adventure every time and we have even discovered the number that will deliver booked train tickets by post. We have tested times and connections and can now book a quiet carriage out and back with tickets to hand - hassle free - and know the watering holes too! Cancelled trains etc just add to the challenge, the biggest is actually getting the detail right when booking.

Just entering third week of treatment, steroids will be adjusted next session to avoid withdrawal symptoms. It was all very intense and I even had pyjamas ready. David and I were travelling down together and I didn't tell him it was in the balance whether I could get there. But 4.30am on the day of travel I was just starting to come round. So up at 6am, gently put things together, just managed a shower then a cross-country drive through the Lincolnshire

Lanes and eventually to Newark Northgate for hot chocolate and The Times. I began to come round as we travelled.

Returning from the appointment we made our way across Black Friar's Bridge and walked down the embankment, passing the cafes and second hand book stalls, Foyles bookshop (already targeted) and on towards the London Eye almost opposite the Houses of Parliament. There we boarded the new Thames River Cruise Service (from under the Eye). A fabulous round trip just relaxing as the lights of London and the River were coming to life. It was utterly magical. The Tower and the Bridges beautifully lit. Tutankhamen was projected onto the roof of the Dome to promote the exhibition beneath and as we surged down the river you could feel the heart of a great world metropolis and sense history and sailing boats and global commerce. Then in we drew in style to catch the train at Black Friar's Bridge.

We discovered a very handy McDonalds near Kings Cross Station before boarding the 7.03pm. After a glass of wine from the trolley for David, I was told it was very civilized. Then slept all the way home!

A great day out and all for the Revlimid Trial.

24 November 2007

THE PILLS

She sat with the bag
A 'lost' look on her face
Where to begin?
Of that NOT a trace
Labels and warnings
Days 1, 4 and 7
Red white and blue ones
A quick trip to heaven
Just where to start
Her courage had failed
Before, after or with
She'd get it all nailed
Out came the blank sheet
And brain into gear
Write it all down
And conquer the fear
We'll start after breakfast
And give it a try
But sickness and heartache
It's all gone awry
So research some info
It shouldn't take long
Where to get help
If things go wrong

Drawing on 'know how'
And ideas abound
The knowledge comes forth
And help can be found
Then brain into gear
And plan out the day
With porridge for breakfast
The Pills slip away
And baked beans at lunch
They're sliding down fast
Three litres of water
And one large pint glass
Prunes before breakfast
Weak Lady Grey tea
Fresh fruit and veg
It's all up to me!

22 November 2007

(See medication chart page 86)

Effective information at handover is priceless

SUNFLOWER
A winning mindset

AN AGE OF MIRACLES

I hope to be very honest next visit about the effects of medication. It is tough the first two weeks and real recovery is in the last two or three days, but it just seems positive to put it behind you and be normal. It is the best advise we ever had. Just get on with life. But I did wonder how getting across London yesterday with torn leg muscles playing up after a frosty fall would turn out. We took it steadily. The Trial results were thrilling, down from 22 to 6 with the first session of treatment. It is so stunning it has taken time to sink in. Never assume, I learned long ago.

Climbing off the train at Blackfriars on the return journey we gently made our way to St Paul's. A Christmas carol service was in progress with the choir and magnificent organ. The vast interior glowed in candlelight and glorious music. We paused. Exquisitely carved stonework. Inspiringly beautiful pictures. The very essence of Christmas. The Blessing. Peace. An endless congregation of all ages and nationality made their way down the aisle. We eventually followed and lit a candle beneath Mary and Jesus with a prayer.

Then sideways down the great steps. Everywhere so exquisitely lit. Starlit trees. Many young people. Photographers. It was all happening. Navigational instinct led across towards a narrow alley, away from the great gates of the City, sloping gently it had to lead back to the Thames. We had arrived by a roundabout route at the east end of the cathedral and thought it was closed. So to finish Christmas with this glorious service was unforgettable. We plunged down the cobbled alleyway, past one or two exciting looking old London pubs. A dogleg to the left and eventually reached a main turning just before Blackfriars. All well noted.

We arrived at St Pancreas - half open really - little shops and Bistros just emerging along the broad Mall between the stations. It is huge, shiny, ultra modern (£800,000,000). Signs had apparently only sprung into operation in the morning. We chatted to a very tall security guard. We admired this amazing modern achievement. He hoped things would keep going - sounded like teething troubles were still being sorted out.

We spotted a cafe with outside tables as we made our way towards Kings Cross through the expanse of glass and elevators. It promised hot soup and there was a free table. We enjoyed a fragrant tomato and herb potage with olive bread.

It was fun. The bustle of travellers and life between stations. The thrill of being part of this 'state of the arts' ongoing development. Eurostar. Change here for Paris, 2 hours 15 minutes. The Continent. Basle another 3 hours 30 minutes. Such wonderfully simple access via the Channel tunnel. Lively baby animals and a giraffe cavorted temptingly around the floor of Hamleys tiny toy shop almost next door. One now awaits a small boy coming to visit from Australia.

Outside the road complex was unfinished. Barriers everywhere. City haste reflected across wet surfaces. No crossing. We breathed in that heady essence of London as we explored our way to Kings Cross in darkness, a 'stones throw' away through the waiting taxis ticking over in expectation, condensing fumes adding to the overall character of life. Richard always said when he was on his way back he could smell the horse muck from Knightsbridge as he climbed off the train!

After a quick visit to the tempting M&S shop we made the 7.30pm.   There was a great rush for the train when details were displayed, then that long walk to our seats in the quiet carriage at the front of the train, even round a bend in the platform. Must count the carriages next time! It had been crammed down the aisles and every available space on the way down. Now, surprisingly, a quiet return.

Richard was waiting for us at Newark Northgate. A fast, gentle journey home. Heavenly.

Thought I would be in real trouble in the morning with the leg injury.   It was extraordinary. The pain had gone.

3 January 2008

THE REVLIMID TRIAL
(Kings College Hospital, Denmark Hill, London and City Hospital Nottingham)

REMISSION

A frosty slip in the garden
flu and a chesty cold
and even a week off to catch up
then **Remission** we were told!
It was an absolute surprise
hadn't given it a thought
for months and years we'd done our best
and here was the news we'd sought.
Sheer joy and pure amazement
Thanks to all who'd taken part
Then on the 'phone to friends and home
who'd battled from the start.
And now for some injections to get me back on track
I've put them all together too
and haven't lost the knack!
May happiness runs through my veins
then stick to the skilful plan
Success is what we've fought for
And we'll crack it if we can!

April 2008

HOPE

And so we quietly battle on
But hope we're getting there
In skilful hands, with skilful plans
Will success be there to share?
As spring turns into summer
We make our trip to town
Three months to go, though bloods are low
Medications coming down!

May 2008

PROVENCE
Wildflowers and a mountain stream, just a sheer delight.

23

OPTIMISM

Optimism is essential
It's a job to get it right
Strength and inspiration
With success in sight
Love and laughter friends and fun
Family big and small
The input of each one of them
Brings happiness to all
They are positive and normal
Fill our lives with love and fun
When told 'Oh I'm OK just now'
Reply 'Thank goodness for that Gran!'

June 2008

HAPPINESS

We made it out to Provence
With not a cloud in sight
Wild flowers and a mountain stream
Just a sheer delight

July 2008
(Revlimid Trial began 7th November 2007)

THE FUTURE

Five years and full remission at fourth treatment, the implications for other patients must be huge. Chemotherapy taken orally at home. Little hair loss. Progress into maintenance therapy is now the challenge.

I wonder if the way medication is taken makes any difference?

What a difference it might have made with earlier diagnosis. If a blood test had been taken when tested for osteoporosis - tingling in the long bones and scalp - only 'wear and tear' was suggested.

Does diet, lifestyle, exercise, effective way of taking drug regime make a difference. Does the support of a busy, caring family and the power of prayer play a part. The time and skill from just everyone is extraordinary and so appreciated.

What an amazing journey

July 2008

(Ninth Session)

Signs before diagnosis

Tingling in long bones and scalp. Mouth infections. Considerable weight loss. Nose bleeds. Two severe bouts of flu with month in bed and antibiotics. Weakness. Could not lift heavy pans. Loss of energy. Tired. Very pale.

THE GLOW OF AUTUMN

As the rich tints of autumn glow through the gardens
and delicate silver birch leaves scatter across freshly mown grass
and bonfires appear in open spaces
and huge rich ripe pumpkins prepare for Halloween
Days are getting shorter, mornings darken into vibrant autumn
It is with us, a sharp gust here and there
The birds are back on the feeder near the kitchen window
We are busy sawing and pruning and tidying
The apples are safely in the shed
But we still had some chicks off today
The garden feels so full of life
Handfuls of raspberries are still to be had
The odd pink campion braves a few blooms
then a perfect rose
Forget-me-nots are growing
but it is a time of transition - suspension - then breathless
until the early bulbs awaken the Spring

October 2008

WITH LUCK

I've had a scan to check the score
And Ganocyte's been stopped
And blood tests once a fortnight now
And walking quite a lot

Recovery has been very slow
But now we're getting there
Blood tests are improving
With fitness is in the air

It's six years since it all began
And many journeys on
Two trials, stem cell, yes four in all
But still we're going strong

Revlimid has been the key
And Kings has been the wonder
So when the PCT turned me down
With luck we found their number

We've travelled down through thick and thin
From winter into summer
And spring is on its way again
Just as I recover

At dusk tonight the birds began
their chorus to the spring
It filled our hearts with gladness
and the hope a new year brings

So back to where it all began
to City before Kings
Just sixty miles to drive from here
To keep an eye on things

Sincere thanks..... January 2009

REVLIMID TRIAL COMPLETE REMISSION 2008
MADE AVAILABLE ON NHS 2009

DAFFODILS AT HOME IN THE SNOW
Gorgeous pristine shining snow, temperatures way down below.

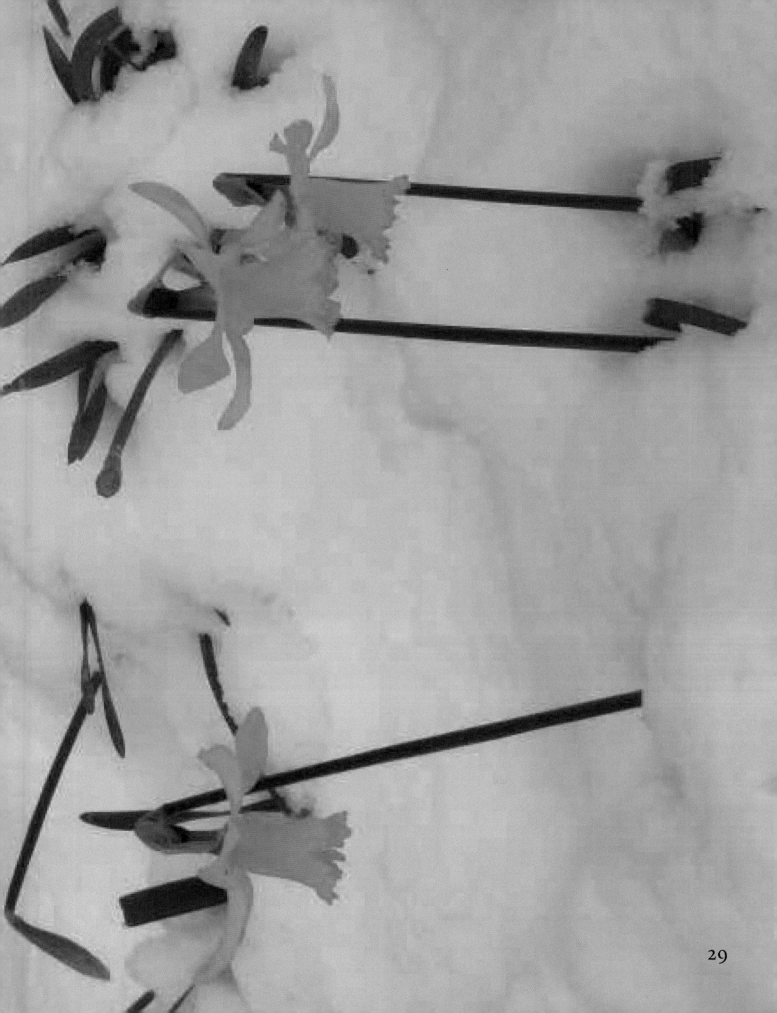

A GOOD MILE

(August 2008 to February 2009)

The end in sight we jumped for joy
Now just to test bone marrow
So brave and strong we chatted on
Then there came tomorrow

Counts plummet low, platelets at ten
So blood tests and infusions
Kindness phone calls GCSF
There was no confusion

Our GP had been on the line
With the information
To hospital at once they said
There's sound communication

I spoke with VJ down at Kings
To let her know the score
Along with Beth she cared for me
I couldn't have asked for more

Maintenance is out I'm told
Stop all medication
'Go home and recover!'
It was a strange sensation

Still full of hope, another fight
to get some platelets back
They certainly caused a challenge
With bruises blue and black

So contact, kindness, T.L.C.
Sheer determination
Have just recorded all of it
Results are quite amazing

Just slowly, slowly things improved
With all the thoughtful care
Input from so many
Results are here to share

So dodging flu and trying hard
I miss my trip to Kings
But you must be seen they tell me
So Dr Williams sorts out things

But tests are up, no Granocyte
Can walk a good mile too
You have to learn to pace yourself
Its all I had to do!

(*For details see appendix iii*)

(Back to Kings 4th March 2009)

DAYBREAK

As dawn comes gently from the night
To hedges fresh with dew
And day is coming into Life
To find a world brand new

Rainbows sparkle from the grass
Spiders webs are laced with jewels
Birds sing joy unto the dawn
Once more Life is renewed

Sunbeams shine through early mist
In the magic of the dawn
Long shadows reach across the earth
So fleetingly - then gone

Every time it is our gift
When rose light fills the sky
And animals begin to stir
And time is just a sigh

To start again with Life so fresh
As a sleeping world unfolds
And radiance lights awakening day
With promises untold

September 2009

FIRELIGHT

As firelight warmed the hearts of a growing family
And candles lit our lives with secret light
And laughter filled the crevices with happiness
And stories filled the night with such delight
And parents and grandparents and cousins
Shared the love a family may hold
And the future held the secrets and the promises
Of young lives beginning to unfold
We relaxed in that glowing firelight
The leaping flames brought light into our souls
The precious moments of a family drawn together
Warmed the future and the stories yet untold

November 2009

A SPECIAL KIND OF GIFT

Time for Time - A Gift for Life

Enthusiasm, optimism, the clear seeing mind of youth. Full of hope and zest for life. Fresh as a flower. What a gift. So much to offer. But a gift we can share, for we too have much to learn and much to give. Why a generation gap? Why not a fine bond of trust and friendship.

Just as a child is our very own creation so we are the beginning of their whole life. All the latent talent and ability is ours to encourage and if we accept our responsibility with loving time and thought, just as any young thing will reveal the quality of its care so our children will blossom into life. An innocent soul with so many thoughts and feelings and loves of their very own. Let us learn to know them and respect and value them for the dear individual that they are and can become.

There is so much to enjoy with a child. Their innocence. Their sincerity. Their humour. Their clear ideas about life. Let us share that joy and guide them gently. For the considered approach of a loving or caring adult who has learned from life and is willing to take the time to pass on the valued lessons assimilated over the years can lay the caring foundations upon which the wonderful gift of life may be built.

The confidence of a sensitive young mind is a fragile and beautiful thing. A key to themselves. Let us never miss it. Never be too busy for the sweetness and joy around us. Let us earn their unquestioning loyalty. The love and respect that cannot be demanded and treasure each golden chance we are given to see their special qualities growing into life. May they bring a closeness and openness within the family that will build a background where children can develop good sense, strength and confidence in which to create their own individual talents for the future.

Let us accept the extra moments we have with our children as a special kind of gift. The times confined by childhood ailments as a chance for a few golden hours of comradeship. A treasured interlude for sharing. A time just to be friends. For time for time is a gift for life and the pleasure of these quiet hours can bring joy, strength and understanding on which to build for the future. With a fresh open and fertile mind all seems possible and this priceless gift is ours to give and ours to share. And who knows we may even rear a bloom of rare beauty.

Tathwell 1970

PAPER WHITE ROSE FROM SARAH
Stillness, that sense of peace, tranquillity, a garden.

ENDLESS SNOW

Spring's emerging once again
After snow and ice and pouring rain
The coldest spell of weather yet
Since recent records have been kept

Gorgeous pristine shining snow
Temperature way down below
Roads snowed up and cars snowed in
And all the neighbours just chipped in

Freezing hard on ice packed roads
No 'gritters' possible we were told
Then rain upon the solid ice
Conditions were not very nice

Elisabeth flew home despite the snow
Main airports already closed
Chicago, Schiphol, Humberside
Then reeking snow, a testing drive

It really did go on and on
Can hardly believe that it has gone
Hay place collapsed with weight of snow
Fifteen degrees and more below

Two feet of snow came sliding down
The boot room roof completely drowned
Assessor came when we were out
Said 'Just get on and sort it out'!!

2010

DELIGHTFUL LITTLE CALL DUCKS PLAYING IN THE SNOW
Elisabeth flew home despite the snow, main airports already closed, Chicago, Schipol, Humberside. Then reeking snow a testing drive.

OVERDRIVE!

Revlimid Treatment began 31 January 2011

Now it is just getting light
And I've been awake all night
Let's hope the pills are working well
And good results are there to tell.
I'm writing, planning, painting too
There seems so much for me to do!
Spring flowers ready to put in pots
Today I've managed all the lot!
But that is steroids. Am aware
So gardened on without a care!
Carried on 'til nearly six
Then there was the tea to fix.
Steroids do cause quite a high
Such energy's good I can't deny
Not much sleep for several days
By Friday I'm in quite a haze
Then manage to sleep on Saturday night
Sunday I'll be feeling right
Tuesday it all starts again
Will be feeling much the same!
Awake at midnight, face aglow
All a bit silly I know
A romantic film late into the night
Let's hope recovery is soon in sight.
So reading, writing - getting lots done
Just 'forty winks' is better than none

Managing to deal with side effects
Wonder what will turn up next?
Tingly, stiff legs for two or three days
Hot baths and walking and time soon erase
Lots of experience helps things along
Then where to get help if things go wrong
Dealt with allergy the very first week
Been given a number for help to seek
An antibiotic not taken before
'Stop, take Piriton your health will restore'
So hot itching scalp had gone in two days
Quick effective response my spirits raised
A phone call and 'bleep' straight to the
source
And at all times, what a priceless resource
Had hoped to be 'stable' after complete
remission
Hope this time I'll reach that happy position
Timing and excellence may be the key
Just the detail is up to me!

17 February 2011

(diagnosis 2003)

REVLIMID TREATMENT - Seven months on:

Weak, hard to recover
Not capable of walking far
Light headed, medicated, fragile
Feel the cold

Felt very fit and walked daily when treatment commenced.
Had huge amounts of energy at beginning and achieved much. Fragile now and have to take
it very steady.
Paraproteins at 2 for three months

• What happens next?
• Will my strength come back?
• Will bloods recover?

• five week appointment if possible ?

August 2011

(Trial steroids much easier to tolerate taken days 1 – 4)

EIGHTH MONTH
and DOWN TO 15mg

Seven months on I hoped to thrive
As steroids tabs were cut to five
And every week still had to take
A dose that kept me wide awake
Results are good, the counts are low
But where's my energy I'd like to know
Can't walk or work, exhausted too
Just wondering really what to do
I started out so fit and well
And decorated for a spell!!
I took so much when on 'The Trial'
But always loved to walk a mile
Just wonder why I'm so knocked back
How soon will I be back on track?

Month eight and down to 15 m g
When will some improvement be?
We're longing to be on our way
We're ready for a holiday
Will try and find what I can do
Then hope to be as good as new!!

September 2011

12.9.2011   HB 12.5   WBC 3.1   Plts 75   Neuts 0.73   Paraproteins 3

Ninth Month begins. Medication stopped for two weeks

(for details see appendix iv)

THISTLE – watercolour
Amongst the beautiful wildflower meadows above the chalk cliffs at Beer, Devon.

16th July 2006
Birk

OH! WHAT A TREAT TO GARDEN AGAIN

What a treat to garden again
Golden and still after overnight rain
Geraniums to store for the summer ahead
Then to replace with wallflowers instead!
Prune back the lavender, tidy loose ends
Ready for spring as winter descends
Rich golden days as leaves change their hue
Shades of red, green and silver, shining with dew
Apples now wrapped and safe in their shed
Tomatoes in chutney for winter ahead
Now pruning is needed for shrubs and for trees
With secateurs and saw, up steps or on knees
Oh what a treat to garden once more
This glorious energy, hope there's lots more in store!

Tuesday 2 November 2011

Fourth Week of MONTH TEN - Steroid day!!

10mg dexomethazone
(15mg Revlimed every other day for 21 days)

(for details – apendix iv)

'KICK ON'

Feeling fit ....!!
But days 1 to 4 go on a bit
And now it is poetry night
Trying hard to get things right!
Mesmerized but on the go
Proteins 6 are still quite low
Dosed 1 to 4 at my request
To get results is quite a test
Thought better have them all in one
Then just get on and have some fun
Get wound up in those four days
Coming round in quite a haze
Prefer to get them out the way
Than every week on just one day
So much vision each decision
Trial achieved complete remission
Will give anything a try
Can be tough I can't deny
And so another 'tweek' begins
Quietly 'KICK ON' and get stuck in ....!!
4 February 2012

(DAY 5)

Dexomethazone Days 1-4 from December 2011
as Clinical Trial - see appendix iv (page 92).

TAKE TIME

Take time to think
It is a source of power
Take time to read
It is the foundation of wisdom
Take time to play
It is the secret of staying young
Take time to be quiet
It is the opportunity to seek God
Take time to be aware
It is the opportunity to help others
Take time to love and be loved
It is God's greatest gift
Take time to laugh
It is the music of the soul
Take time to be friendly
It is the road to happiness
Take time to dream
It is what the future is made of
Take time to pray
It is the greatest power on earth
There is a time for everything

(treasured poem – unknown source)

SWANS AT PASTURE LANE
Take time to dream. It is what the future is made of.

44

ENDLESS CARE

Eventually diagnosed February 2003
September to February it took to see
I needed care as weight fell away
Had blood test but NO results so thought all was ok
So weakness and nose bleeds and couldn't lift pans
Getting quite thin and pale and wan
Then in February I rang clinic seven
Ali's response 'Can you come in the morning?'
I knew that it had to be serious then
So now a bone marrow, and blood tests again
'You are a strong woman' the Consultant said
Take all the pills before going to bed
A long wait at pharmacy and so it began
Patiently waiting would soon learn the plan
We read all the labels in front of the fire
Took so many pills before we retired
Was soon back on a ward quite overwhelmed
David was there, thought it was the end!
Was told should have been on HDU
David asked questions it was all he could do

Seeking knowledge and answers is such a key part
It was just a blank page so where do you start?
To Leicester by mini bus for a plasma change
Instead of an ambulance that had been arranged
Hooked to a machine chatting pleasantly there
Woke with patches all over and bed end in the air!
Projectile vomited on the way back
Then under Sisters window until back on track
There are angels about they always shine
We're eternally grateful for their wisdom and time
From Lincoln and Leicester, then Nottingham and Kings
All along the way we've learned a few things
A Stem Cell, two Drug Trials and treatment once more
Clarity emerges when you know the score
The family are brilliant and switched on too
No matter what it is they always 'will do'
They keep us in touch their lives are so full
With text, phones and visits life's never dull
They have been awesome and shared it all
With such endless kindness I've loved it all

Thank you ....

THE SIMPLE BASICS

I have learned it is the 'simple basics' that are so effective. And 'Just be normal' was the best advise we were ever given.

Settling in to a routine and getting your head round treatment takes a few days. But what may have seemed *mind bogglingly* complicated soon becomes routine. Initial reaction recedes.

Try to leave first appointment with effective information about how to take medication (then read enclosed leaflets and highlight relevant information – it's easy to refer back later if needed). Knowledge is healing to yourself and helpful to those caring for you. Choosing whether to share it becomes clear after a few days too. Learn to know your medication inside out so you can be as meticulous as possible.

Take treatment carefully as advised. Write it down 'simply' and stick to it. Making up a seven day pack of medication may be helpful.

Having a contact number for help at all times brings comfort and reassurance.

Fluids and diet are key. They keep the system moving. It helps enormously if you can avoid the stress of constipation whilst on medication. I take two or three litres of fluid daily. Water/fruit juice/ weak tea/fruity tea etc. Prunes and all-bran at breakfast keep the system moving. Prunes any time! Plenty of fresh fruit and veg and salads work wonders.

Deal with any nick or injury immediately. Avoids infection. Gloves are helpful. Eye drops solved my sensitive eye problems.

If not sleeping music is wonderfully soothing. Books, magazines, writing, radio, diary (so helpful for reference). A good late night film! As long as warm, relaxed and resting all aid recovery. I find my own little room great in the middle of the night. Cups of tea etc don't disturb anybody!

Exercise is so important. Walking seems to be a great tonic for mind and body and the dogs love it too! I enjoy gardening and find it peaceful and creative. Painting, sewing, reading, cooking, baking, just anything that is satisfying and gives a sense of joy and achievement. We drive a pony and trap. I walk up steep hills. Activity aids sleep! Hot soak in the bath, refreshing shower aids circulation. The care and company of family and friends - phone calls, letters, emails, skype - all aid recovery and promote peace of mind.

It is a challenge. The whole picture is a balance. If you make mistakes learn from them! If you have good ideas, share them. Communication is vital.

Every time it is different. Every case different. Every response different. Outlook and application different. But this has worked for me. Never take anything for granted. Have questions written down for your consultant well in advance. Leave nothing to chance.

GOOD LUCK.

2012

DON'T STAND ABOUT!!

I really cannot stand about

It just seems to knock me out

Can cook and garden and love to walk

But cannot stand about and talk!

Gives me tingly legs or feet

So usually carry a nifty seat

Or try to find a handy perch

Never have very far to search

If I get caught it is a fact

It really does knock me back

So I must be very tough

And sit down when I've had enough

So that is the battle plan

Don't stand about – sit if you can!!

March 2012

WARTS AND ALL

Poetry Day! - Day Five

Kings Revlimid Trial began
7 November 2007

Notts Revlimid Treatment
began 31 January 2011

Spoke with clinic yesterday
Proteins down to five
It's so extraordinary really
And so good to be alive!

Gardened all the morning
With vision and with leisure
Raking, pruning, weeding, moving
Now I've got its measure

Helebores are out
As beautiful as can be
Central spinney's full of light
As RIK has pruned the trees

Daffodils just coming through
To keep the snowdrops company
Our lovely birds are here in droves
As they sort out nesting country

Midge galloped round the lawn today
And left her fairy tracks
Truffle's due for puppies
Must sort stud dogs and facts

Feel so very clear minded
Unbelievably enlightening
Diary at my finger tips
Some details are quite frightening

Clarity emerges
When you know the score
Research is ongoing
Who could ask for more

As I study diaries
It's so very clear to see
'Warts and all' recorded
And it happened to ME

3 March 2012

Revlimid - *Days 1 to 21 - 10mg*
Dexamethazone - *Days 1-4 10mg*

A MARATHON TO SUCCESS

Right from the heart

'Just stick at it'!!

What an extraordinary effect steroids have. A wind up on mind and body and then having to keep warm, calm and gentle to come round and recover, avoiding emotional reaction. Really just go into neutral. Nothing controversial and just come round. Laxative food and lots of fluids to keep the system moving is an essential key to success. Balanced exercise before and after.

If anyone told you when you were diagnosed, what would you make of it? The only way to know is to experience it and keep learning.

I have tried to record with poetry and humour and honesty. Coming out of the haze on day six it will take until at least Wednesday to recover. So then two and a half weeks of 'normal' rather than two days out of seven when taken weekly. You need quiet caring and 'switched on' sense. 'Just be normal'. The first and wisest advice we ever had.

What a marathon. Two successful Drugs Trials and Stem Cell Transplant. Five sessions in all.

Now proteins checked at five by Revlimid and Dexamethazone and the challenge of a settled regime after a year of getting there . I hope to have achieved a 'stable' regime and will just 'stick at it'!!

Thanks to you all.   Day six 'Recovering' .   Sunday 4 March 2012

TEAZLE - watercolour - A painting is the spirit of a human being in relationship to a sense of place. The human mind that sometimes presumes there is no such thing as a miracle is itself a miracle.

BACK ON TRACK

'Sun, Sea and Walsingham'

SESSION SIXTEEN - WEEK TWO

2 April 2012

(Revlimid 10mg Days 1 to 21 - Dexamethazone 10mg x 4 Days 1 - 4)

Back to Nottingham.

Low neutrophils (0.62) at last week's appointment. Nivestim injections already in fridge. 2.30pm appointment for blood tests to see if injections needed.   Wondering if I would have to come off treatment. Much improved since beginning **Dexamethazone on days 1 to 4 from 5 December 2011.**

Rested and relaxed completely to try and give bloods every chance to recover. We had a delightful day on the Norfolk coast Wednesday and a visit to Walsingham in hot sunshine. Parked at the Farm Shop. Dick stayed with Truffle. It was too hot to leave her in the car. Bought a fresh Norfolk cauliflower. The gardens were immaculate as always. Beautiful fragrant shades of blue and white. A gardener with flowing robes was cutting the grass in great style with a ride-on lawn mower. Thought of all the family.

We enjoyed seafood from Cley on Salthouse beach. Rum and raisin ice cream on Wells harbour with the Brent geese. Tea in glorious light amongst the boats at Overy Staithe.   I felt healed.

Amazing. Bloods recovering.

(Nivestim30 MU/0.5ml injections x 2 weekly begin 23 April 2012 (after a week off)

SESSION EIGHTEEN - 28 MAY 2012

Dexomethazone 8mg x 4 Days 1-4 from 28 May (2 tablets with food breakfast and teatime) **Revlimid 10mg Days 1-21 of each 28 day cycle** (at night). **Nivestim x 2 weekly** *(Monday and Thursday at night).*   **Lansoparole 30mg** (hour before breakfast). **Aspirin 75mg daily** (with food).   **Bonefos 800mg daily** (10.30am and 10.30pm - an hour before or after food). Magnesium 250mg (daily with food). Multivitamins.

HB 12.3   WBC 4.52   Platelets 130   Neutrophils 1.69   Paraproteins 5

DAYS WITHOUT END

Good results once more tonight

And we've brought in the exercise bike!

Intend to deal with legs quite dizzy

Bike in Norfolk kept me busy

Sea and sunshine did the rest

And sunburned legs a surprising test!

But seemed to work so pedalling on

Determination going strong

Now caravan ready for Burghley next week

For Elisabeth and boys – a special treat

Rob put up the bunks, so tucked in tight

Sarah brought the caravan then it rained overnight

New ground sheet for awning was a birthday treat

Don't know how many we're going to sleep

So all of the children were soon gathering there

A memorable event we had so often shared

And David came with his motor bike too

Alarm went off and put small boys in a stew!!

In Norfolk little cousins and tents came along

Mud sliding and sea dipping all day - on and on

Crabbing off the pier, swam as tide coming in

Then back round the boats

Days without end ....August 2012

BURNHAM OVERY STAITHE HARBOUR ACROSS THE SEA LAVENDER
Crabbing off the pier, swam as tide coming in then back round the boats, days without end.

HIGH SUMMER

The sweetest thing in life could be

To sit beneath the cooling trees

The sun beats down, the garden stirs

And dances in the fragrant air

The dogs stretch out around my feet

And nettles wilt in midday heat

And birdsong fills this summer day

Their young so gently hide away

And butterflies and breezes roam

This lovely place that we call

HOME

!!MOVING!!

Spring 2013

Exciting things happening
As we gently thrive
Invited near family
Share their very busy life

But there's so much to tackle
To take it on board
Agents, viewing and moving
And sorting the hoard......

Of endless treasures
Gathered over the years
Now such lively plans
Begin to appear!

Snowdrops and aconites
Are peeping through
All the stirrings of Life
So much to do

Family brimming with sense
Want us at hand!
Move quietly near them
Such exciting plans

Pony and dogs and
Changes abound
Bunk beds for sleepovers
Keep safe and sound

We're really quite fragile
For a challenging move
Will start sorting out
All the above

Life's full of endeavour
Gathered over the years
So will 'keep kicking on'
See what appears!!.....

EVENING FLIGHT

As evening draws in
From an endless day's sun
We drive over the stubbles
Terrier's off for a run

From the pony and trap
We are in close touch
With the essence of wildlife
We love so much

Sunset is near
When they finally arrive
This glorious spectacle
From the evening sky

One of nature's miracles
This magical sound
Echoing over the hills
But Truffle's around!

The geese pause in their quest
Changing their plan
Calling, circling, then settling
Before their nights feed begins

Just beyond the hedge
Where the sun sinks in the west
The combine has left them
A glorious feast

So we trot home
Over darkening hills
Part of the glory
Of harvest fulfilled

August 2013

HARVEST TIME WITH MIDGE AND TRUFFLE
From the pony and trap we are in close touch with the essence of wildlife we love so much.

SUNRISE

'Thorntree Cottage'

We're here, we've survived!
Can't fit it all in, but
Sunrise surrounds us
As daylight seeps in

Over the fields
Stretching all round
This beautiful vision
Was here to be found

And in the evening
Towards the north east
The cathedral is glowing
As daylight retreats

Then a knock and a visit
Any time of the day!
And farm life over the hedge
As they work this way

So observing the world
From inside out
Is a delightful bonus
As it turns out...

November 2013

THOSE FEW PRECIOUS MINUTES

Consultant Appointment - 'The Vital Link'

Those few precious minutes
The key to success
Details to gather
Thoughts to express

Those few precious minutes
To study the case
Consider the facts
Not a moment to waste

The knowledge and skill
Conveyed at this time
Are crucial to progress
Keep treatment in line

Those few precious minutes
To take it all in
Ask questions and listen
A challenge to win

Life's in the balance
Such skill is at hand
Store every detail
Be constructive with plans

So record and remember
Or share with a friend
To recapture the content
It helps no end

Don't miss the moment
Seek positive advice
Those few precious minutes
A key to your life.......

ANTIBIOTICS ON STANDBY?

Knocked back by treatment
Infection on chest
A very upset tum
A challenge.....I guess

Going down hill
At the weekend
Had antibiotic for emergency
What a 'godsend'

Then sorting tum
But gunk stuck on chest
Rough for two weeks
Getting distressed

Phone call to surgery
Understood my plight
Chest still a problem
Help is in sight!

Kindly put out medication
For 6pm
Hoping still 'stable'
Will kick on........again!

Kindness, communication
All play their part
Timing so vital
Right from the start

Antibiotic for emergency
Did save the day
When help needed at weekend
Some more tucked away

Sincere thanks
May 2014

WILDLIFE AT GLANFORD FORD
We love to pause at the ford bringing back childhood memories of hours spent dabbling in a crystal clear stream.

MUD ON YOUR BOOTS

Norfolk Coastal Path - Sea and Islands - To Scolt Head from Brancaster

Thursday 18 September 2014 Away by 10.45. An amazingly easy run down the A15 and A17 towards Kings Lynn. It is over two years since we have been to Norfolk (with Norfolk terriers) and the sun came out, hot and golden and Eliza phoned.

We picnicked before a visit to Walsingham. Tall grasses shone against the light with exquisite cosmos, the blues of asters, amazing ice plants with variegated leaves and here and there a perfect dahlia. The garden is always a triumph and the gardener said it was ok for Truffle. So we shared a seat and took it in turns to light a candle and Richard brought water from the well. Then across country.

We paused at the lovely Wiverton ford bringing back childhood memories of endless hours spent dabbling in a crystal clear stream that disappears under the bridge and across the fields. Then a visit to the art gallery at Cley and a purchase of 'Nightscapes' and a delicate silver spoon. On to Salthouse where the car park has been taken over by shingle and stones and grand undulating banks but the fishermen were still there! After a call at the Old Post Office for Elisabeth's birthday card and some homemade flapjack we worked our way along the coast, round the harbours at Blakeney and Wells and onto the much loved tide washed beach at Overy Staithe.   Finally we reached our garden room with a warm greeting and a tiny flask of cold milk for tea and eventually wandered down in floating mist over the bridge onto the coastal path to the seat by the lobster pots.

Friday Tea at 6am. Onto a hazy shore with Truffle before breakfast. A curlew, noisy redshanks, oyster catchers, teal and a few brent geese - just starting to arrive - were feeding or quietly resting. A morning of still, beautiful life. Hugh Brandon-Cox's treasured book 'Mud on my Boots' came to mind. Sketched on the shore after breakfast. A pastel of lobster pots. It evoked the feel of marsh and water and vast open spaces. How could the tide reach here? But there

was the tide line recorded four or five feet up on the old shed at the side of the path.

We were soon away to buy anchovies from the fish shop for Richard and local blueberries which are perfectly delicious and then drove on to Overy Staithe for a picnic lunch on the beach. Beautiful deep coloured reflections of the boats shone in the water. I walked the high bank with Truffle. Lots of Redshanks about and the Egrets were busy along the shore. We shared greetings with dogs and walkers enjoying the path. Then back for a wildlife cruise at 3.30pm.

We met up with a local mussel fisherman and were soon away through the boats and bouys towards Scolt Head Island. History and information were imparted as we explored. Having grounded once or twice we eventually pulled ashore and paused to take it all in. Low tides this week. But we reached a remote creek on Scolt Head and made our way across a richly perfumed carpet of sea asters, deep red sea-blite and late lavender and up to the wardens house through dunes of wiry marram grass and on up the steep steps between banks of luscious, ripe, blackberries right to the top. It was magical and misty and we didn't really have the views but it was remote and lovely and we could just see the little boat in the creek where Richard had stopped to relax.

So back towards Brancaster Staithe with a look at the mussel and cockle boats that hoover their catch off the bottom and more local knowledge of the oysters beneath us that are brought in tiny finger nail size to grow on until they are ready for the table. Back to shore for 6pm as the lights were coming up. I was totally disorientated on the way out around the boats and sand banks but eventually worked out east from west and took photos of Brancaster from the sea. Now a quick turn round and a quiet table with an awe inspiring view outwards across shimmering silver water. The tide was up where the mud flats and creeks had been so full of wildlife this morning and the view over the coastal path towards luminous clouds and an endless sparkling sea was breathtaking.

Saturday Richard was down on the beach with Truffle before 7am. We are just relaxing and soaking it all in. Walked right handed down the coastal track before breakfast. Met lots of friendly dog walkers and a round Norfolk relay staging post as runners clocked in. Lots of fun and smiles and support. We saw

EARLY MORNING. TIDE OUT. NORFOLK COASTAL PATH.
Onto a hazy shore before breakfast. Wildfowl just beginning to arrive. Resting. Feeding. A morning of still beautiful life.

them at Overy Staithe later. Tested smoked salmon and scrambled eggs for a late breakfast. Then a quiet run into Burnham Market and the book shop. After a good browse invested in a great little book 'Keep Calm and Carry On'! Onto Plum Farm for supplies - plums, apple juice and sweet plum vinegar. Then Burham Norton and a visit to Nelson's church. We discovered a superb tiny glass studio in the farm buildings. They create their designs and teach in this exciting rural studio. Many exquisite pieces. Purchased a glass and silver moulded clam shell, it is beautiful, a keepsake for a memorable visit, a holiday treasure. Richard collected chestnuts to grow at Thorntree Cottage.

Three days have sped by. We have visited our favourite haunts and it seems like yesterday since we were here. Thinking of walking to Overy Staithe tomorrow morning along the coastal path. We have really revelled in the loveliness of the open marshes, the birds and flowers and quiet beauty of the peace and space. Havn't had sun but it has been still and warm and misty. Walked to a very busy Brancaster Staithe along the coastal path this afternoon and spotted Jon Brown's boat! Hope we can be back again very soon to see the wildfowl coming in to winter on our shores. It is an enthralling sight to see thousands of birds coming in. An experience of a lifetime. High tide at dusk would be natures gift. But luck plays such a great part.

Sunday Richard was on the shore at first light to stretch Truffle's legs. We had dined early last night with another stunning view of water and islands stretching away in the fading light. I walked down to the shore with the camera before we started to pack. Tide out. Muddy creeks. Birds and the life of the sea shore all around through the early mist; and as the sun crept through filling the shore with sunshine and shadows beautiful light lit the horizon.

21 September 2014

73

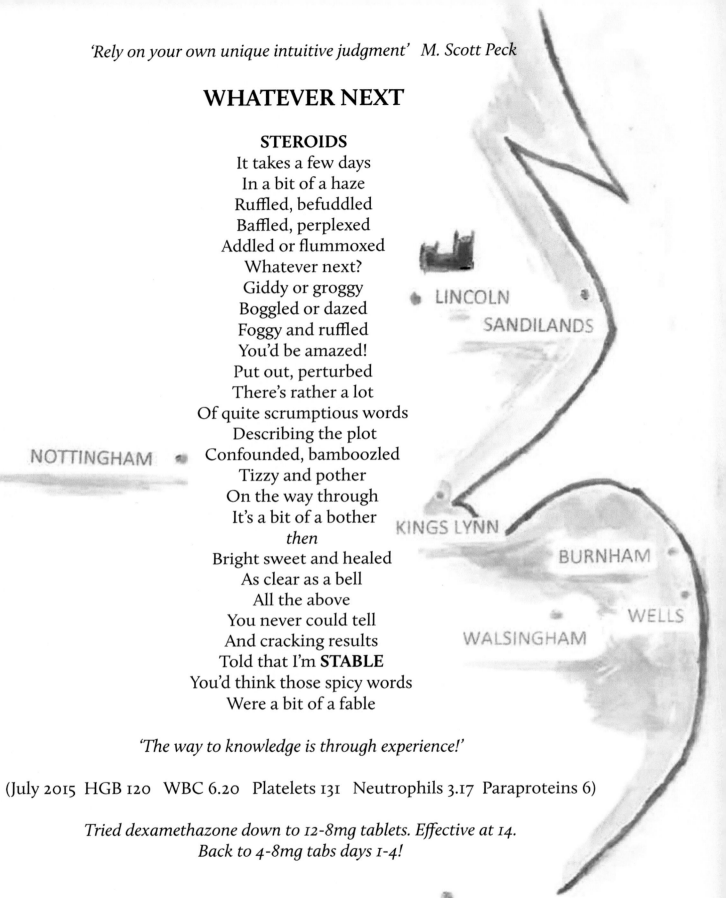

'Rely on your own unique intuitive judgment' M. Scott Peck

WHATEVER NEXT

STEROIDS
It takes a few days
In a bit of a haze
Ruffled, befuddled
Baffled, perplexed
Addled or flummoxed
Whatever next?
Giddy or groggy
Boggled or dazed
Foggy and ruffled
You'd be amazed!
Put out, perturbed
There's rather a lot
Of quite scrumptious words
Describing the plot
Confounded, bamboozled
Tizzy and pother
On the way through
It's a bit of a bother
then
Bright sweet and healed
As clear as a bell
All the above
You never could tell
And cracking results
Told that I'm **STABLE**
You'd think those spicy words
Were a bit of a fable

'The way to knowledge is through experience!'

(July 2015 HGB 120 WBC 6.20 Platelets 131 Neutrophils 3.17 Paraproteins 6)

Tried dexamethazone down to 12-8mg tablets. Effective at 14.
Back to 4-8mg tabs days 1-4!

TURNSTONES - THEY LOVE TO SIT ON THE BOATS
Tide turning. Timing crucial. Vegetation just beginning to reappear.
(Such a delightful sight almost forgot to record the experience - just had to unclude hazy result)

Revlimid Treatment began January 2011

Monday 22 September 2014
Nottingham Appointment 10.10 am

Revlimid Treatment Session **47** begins

Revlimid 10mg Days 1-28.
Dexamethazone 8mg x 4 Days 1-4
Lansoprazole 30mg. Aspirin 75mg.
Bonofos 800mg x 2 daily. Nivestim injection weekly. Magnesium 250mg daily.
Multivitamins.

WBC 4.80 HGB 115 Platelets 132 Neutrophils 2.01
Paraproteins 5

STABLE
(week off)

Monday 7 September 2015
Revlimid Treatment Session **59** begins

WBC 6.8 HGB 125 Platelets 130 Neutrophils 3.1
Paraproteins 6

STABLE

Diagnosis Lincoln	Feb 2003
Stem Cell Nottingham	Oct 2004
Velcade Trial Notts	Sept 2006
Revlimid Trial Kings, London	Nov 2007

Complete Remission

Revlimid Treatment Nottingham began January 2011

Monday 5 October 2015

Revlimid Treatment SESSION **60**

OVER THE TIDE

25 September 2015

Called at Walsingham in lovely sunshine to say thank you. Was cheerfully asked if I would put it in writing. 'Another Spring' is my thank you.

1 October 2015 - Brancaster

Off 7.30 for 8am. Tide up and coming in. We sailed over the marshes and creeks, an endless vista of sparkling sea. It was breathtaking to be on top of the tide, highest for a long time. Calm. Beautiful. Full of Life. A spoonbill. Brent geese and pinkfeet. Widgeon. Redshank, curlew and egret poking about as the water rose. Wildfowl coming in high overhead - early this year.

We landed on the steps at Scolt Head. Had made our way through tough, fragrant Sea Lavender last year. We climbed up by the Warden's House, shared a handful of brambles and soaked in the glorious views of the distant horizon. We photographed Turnstones on the way back, they like to sit on the boats. Tide turning. Timing crucial. Vegetation just beginning to reappear.

Walked down to the harbour with Truffle in the evening. Low tide. Mellow light. Wandered down to the jetty where much crabbing has taken place.   Had experienced the full lunar eclipse on Monday night in a velvety star filled sky. Crystal clear. Still. Luminous. Timeless. The deepest pink glow slowly returning to pale moonlight. Now I walked back to put the final touches to a holiday water colour. Soon to go on the kitchen wall.

SESSION 60

begins 5 October 2015

(Twelve and a half years since diagnosis)

78

OVER THE TIDE - OVERY STAITHE
Tide highest for a long time. Calm. Beautiful. Full of life. Wildfowl poking about as the water rose.
More arriving overhead. Early this year.

THE HEALING POWER OF A DIARY

The Miracle of the Human Mind

A diary reveals those events and details tucked away and the miracle of the human mind brings them back again crystal clear. It seems to be healing to recall the events of the day whilst they are fresh and new. The detail may be lost later but they are all there on the page to recall if needed. It is amazing to spark the memory. The knowledge seems to put life on a sound foundation and it really is very interesting to recall thoughts and events later. But 'just be normal' is still one of the best pieces of advice we ever received. It is a huge strength.

We have moved near the family and are working on creating a new home and garden. Everything is full of life and colour.

The grandchildren are regular visitors and all comes to life in the diary.

mmk

2016

SUNSET - THOSE MAGICAL MOMENTS
Walked down to the harbour. Low tide. Mellow light. Experienced the full lunar exclipse Monday night (28 9 2015 3am)
in a velvety star filled sky. Crystal clear. Still. Luminous. Timeless. The deepest glow returning to pale moonlight.

APPENDIX

THE PROMISE OF SPRING

Spring is round the corner
We are very nearly there
Sharp sparkling frost and sunshine
Golden aconites suddenly stir

It's only early January
The trimmings are just down
But we know that spring is coming
When snowdrops can be found

They are only just emerging
Tiny spears of silvery green
They always hesitate a while....
Then magically we seem

To have a garden full of promise
Purple crocus peeping through
It fills my heart with endless joy
Once more Life is renewed

(my very favourite time of year)

2016

SNOWDROPS IN JANUARY
We know that Spring is coming when Snowdrops can be found

WHAT IS MYELOMA?   -   15 people are diagnosed in the UK every day   -

Myeloma is an increasingly common cancer of the plasma cells. Plasma cells are found in the bone marrow and are a type of white blood cell, part of the immune system, and help to protect the body from infection by producing antibodies.   In Myeloma, a single defective plasma cell (a Myeloma cell) multiplies rapidly producing a single type of antibody, known as paraprotein which has no useful function. Most of the complications and side effects of myeloma are caused by the build- up of abnormal plasma (myeloma) cells in the bone marrow and the presence of paraprotein in the body. Myeloma usually appears in several areas of the body, which is why it is sometimes referred to as multiple myeloma.

DID YOU KNOW? The most common symptoms of myeloma include bone pain, recurring infection, kidney damage and fatigue. Not everyone will experience all or any of these. It can be effectively treated but it cannot yet be cured.

There are approximately 5,700 new cases of myeloma every year in the UK.

It is the second most common form of blood cancer but only represents 2% of all cancers. Public awareness is low. Myeloma mostly affects people over 65 but has been diagnosed in people as young as 20.

Improvement in treatment has meant that survival rates in myeloma are increasing at the fastest rate amongst all cancer types in the UK.

The causes of myeloma are not fully understood but it is thought to be caused by interactions between genetic and environmental factors.

Myeloma UK's goal is to find a cure.

*FOR INFORMATION AND SUPPORT   -   **Myeloma** Infoline 0800 980 3332*

Email AskThe Nurse@myeloma.org.uk or visit www.myeloma.org.uk

***Maggie's** support anyone affected with cancer at any stage and their families and friends. Everyone is welcome at Maggie's. www.maggiescentres.org.*

King's College Hospital NHS

NHS Foundation Trust

DEPARTMENT OF HAEMATOLOGICAL MEDICINE

C.P.A Accredited
Consultant: Dr. S. Schey
Tel: 020 3299 4550
Fax: 020 3299 3514
Clinic/Appts: 020 3299 3334
Date: 20 September 2007

Consultants
Professor G J Mufti
Professor S L Thein
Dr A Pagliuca
Dr R Arya
Dr S Devereux
— Dr S Schey —

Dr R M Ireland
Dr A Mijovic
Dr D Rees
Dr S Height
Dr M Awogbade
Dr A Ho
Dr R Patel

King's College Hospital
Denmark Hill
London SE5 9RS

Tel: 020 3299 9000
Fax: 020 3299 3445
www.kch.nhs.uk

Dear Mrs Knott

Further to our recent telephone conversation, please find attached details of how to get to King's College Hospital for your appointment with Dr Schey on Wednesday 10 October at 2pm. I have attached a National Rail timetable with different time options. I suggest option 4 or 5 to get you here in time for your appointment.

I spoke to Dr Schey about whether you would be able to start treatment on the day and unfortunately he said you will definitely not be able to start on 10 October as you will need to be assessed in clinic and he will discuss with you all the options we have available. I hope this is satisfactory and should you require further information, please do not hesitate to contact me.

With kind regards.

Yours sincerely,

Judith

Judith Aben, Personal Assistant to
Dr Stephen Schey
Consultant Haemato-Oncologist

encs

(iii)

40 TABLETS TO BE TAKEN ON DAYS 1 AND 8   " HAS WORKED FOR ME "

MEDICINE (Name, Strength & Form)	AMOUNT TO BE TAKEN					REASON FOR MEDICATION / ADDITIONAL INFORMATION
	Morning	Midday	Afternoon	Evening	Bedtime	
REVLIMID 25mg DAYS 1-21					AT NIGHT — 9/10pm ✓	
CYCLOPHOSPHAMIDE 700mg DAY ONE + DAY 8	14 TABLETS					TAKEN WITH LUNCH + DOMPERIDONE (B.BEANS & REEF (U))
DEXAMETHASONE 20mg (2ND) 1-4 "FIRST SESSION" 8-11	WITH BREAKFAST — WITH PORRIDGE					10 TOILETS END OF GREEN TEA "PRUNES" TAKEN BEFORE BREAKFAST — DAILY LAXATIVE — EFFECTIVE!!
ALLOPURINOL 300mg ONE DAILY (FIRST SESSION ONLY)	✓					STOPS SIDE EFFECTS OF CYCLOPHOSPHAMIDE
OMEPRAZOLE 20mg ONE DAILY	✓					PROTECTS STOMACH
ASPIRIN 75mg	✓					WITH BREAKFAST PORRIDGE — STOP CLOTTING
DOMPERIDONE 10mg AS NEEDED	ONE ✓					ONE WITH DEXO (STEROIDS) (1-4) (8-11) + ONE WITH CYCLOPHOSPHAMIDE ON 1 & 8 DAYS
BONEFOS (SODIUM CLODRONATE) 800mg x 2	✓					HALF HOUR EITHER SIDE OF FOOD / DRINK?
ACICLOVIR 200mg x 4 DAILY	✓	✓		✓	✓	ANTI VIRAL
CO-TRIMAZOLE 400mg			2 TABS x2 MON PM & THURS AM		✓	PROPHYLACTIC
CENTRUM MULTIVITAMINS & MINERALS				✓ (WITH SUPPER)		

(7 DAY PHOSPHAN " WITH DAILY "LIFTOUTS" TO CARRY TABLETS IN POCKET VERY HELPFUL MAKING UP A)

REVLIMID CLINICAL TRIAL "KINGS' LONDON"
4 WEEK (28 DAY) CYCLE.
SPREADING THE CHEMO. DRUGS ACROSS THE DAY (WITH FOOD)   MYELOMA TRIAL 7.11.200?   "REVLIMID" TRIAL

REVLIMID CLINICAL TRIAL

Kings College Hospital. Denmark Hill, London, SE5 9RS.
Mavis Mary Knott (began 7 November 2007)

Wed 9 July 2008 - To KINGS - NINTH MONTH BEGINS

New Doctor in charge of Trial patients and I was her first patient.   Neutrophils 2.5 - Paraproteins zero. Said no 'Granocyte 43' injections next month (last two months Granocyte twice weekly).   Bone marrow end of ninth month to assess progress.   Blood pressure 110/65.   Revlimid at 15 mg.   Taking it easy this month as injections have been stopped and trying for good results.   It is 'the last fence' this month, must tackle it like the first one!

Wed 6th August 2007 – To Kings – end of ninth month - bone marrow appointment

Neutrophils down to **0.6**   Have come home with x 3 granocyte.

Thursday 7 August 2008   Dr VJ rang. Take injection today, Saturday and Tuesday.   Have a blood test at GP on Monday and fax results to Kings.

Friday 8th August - bonemarrow site aches.

(Sunday 10th to Pony Club Camp prize giving.   12 August to Beach with strawberry cream cake for birthday tea with family)

Thursday 14 August 2008 – To Kings – Saw Dr VJ.   MAINTENANCE begins at 15mg.   **Zero** proteins. Bone marrow site painful.   VJ suggested trying ice.

20 August 2008   **WBC 1.8 - Neutrophils 0.54   -   Platelets 21**

Thursday 21 2008 Dr VJ rang 8.45am **STOP REVLIMID** would ring Dr Read. Collect Granocyte at 4.30pm. Take twice weekly.   Have blood test Tuesday 26th. Walked at Silver Street. Feeling better. Seem to have reached an impasse. Paraproteins at zero. In remission, but bloods have to recover enough to take maintenance therapy. Wonder if Revlimid will be tried at lower dose. Pony Club ride at Westfield tomorrow.

23 August 2008. Had felt a bit fragile for a couple of days.   'Pins and needles'. Said to RIK 'If I feel faint ring VJ'. She rang and said 'if breathless go to local hospital'.   Research had said bring back any unused Revlimid.   I wonder if they knew?

Tuesday 26 August 2008   **HB 10.6 WBC 2.3 - Platelets 14 - Neutrophils 0.38**

Wed 27 August 2008   Spoke with VJ. **STOP ASPRIN AND SEPTRIN.**   And take Granocyte today and tomorrow and blood test Friday. Dr Read rang tonight to check on progress.   **Dr Schey on holiday.**

Thurs 28 August 2008. Took Granocyte injection. Very bad bruising today. Rash - red pinspots appearing on legs from knee to ankle. Purpura spots first on right leg, then on left. Walked at Silver Street.

Friday 29 August 2008.   9am Blood Test at Horncastle.   Dr Read rang 4pm **(platelets under 10)**.   Rang VJ at Kings.   She wanted Lincoln County telephone number and Dr Read's number.   Dr Caroline rang from Waddingworth Ward.   Be in by 5pm.   **Platelets** have to come from Sheffield.   Infusion 11.30 pm - 12.15.   Appointment arranged at Day Care for Monday 11am.   Bruising inside of wrists.   Right hand   5" long by 1 ½" wide.   Left hand 3 ½" x ¾".

Saturday 30 August 2008.   Home   9.30am   Rash on legs fading.

Sunday 31 August 2008.   To the beach with family for Wedding Anniversary.   Children's day.   Endless time in the sea and digging holes.   Still bruising to wrists and canula site.

Monday 1 September 2008.   To Lincoln for blood test.   **Platelets up to 38.**

Friday 5 September 2008.   Lincoln.   Bloods 10am.   **Platelets 17.**   Wait at hospital for platelets.

Wednesday 10 September 2008.   **To KINGS.   Saw Dr Steve Schey.   STOP ALL MEDICATION**

Sunday Hunter Trial at West Ashby.   Ellie Charlie and Henrietta rode and placed.

Monday 15 Sept 2008.	**HB 9.4 – WBC 4.9 – Platelets 14 – Neutrophils 2.73 - 3pm Platelets**
Tuesday 23 Sept 2008.	**HB 8.9 – WBC 2.2 – Platelets 29 – Neutrophils 1.03**
1 December 2008.	**Platelets 60** Granocyte (GCSF) weekly
16 December 2008.	**HB 11.5 - WBC 3.1 – Platelets 73 – Neutrophils 1.33**
29 December 2008.	**HB 11.8 – WBC 2.7 – Platelets 78 – Neutrophils 1.2**
7 January 2009.	**Stop** GCSF (Granocyte) Blood Test fortnightly

Monday 12 January 2009.   To Nottingham.   Dr Cath Williams said 'They knew if anyone could do it, it would be me!'   Bloods recovering.   Off GCSF.   Back to Nottingham in a fortnight to make sure all OK.   Walked down Silver Street and round the big lake for the first time and did not even notice the exercise.

19 January 2009.	Back on **BONEFOS.**
26 January 2009.	**HB 12.5 - WBC 4.01 - Platelets 97 - Neutrophils 1.65 - PP 3**

REVLIMID MADE AVAILABLE ON THE N.H.S. 2009

DEPARTMENT OF HAEMATOLOGICAL MEDICINE
C.P.A Accredited

Consultant: Dr. S. Schey
Tel: 020 3299 4550
Fax: 020 3299 3514
Clinic/Appts: 020 3299 3334
Clinic Date: 12 November 2008
Date: 13 November 2008

Consultants
Professor G J Mufti
Professor S L Thein
Professor J Marsh
Dr A Pagliuca
Dr R Arya
Dr S Devereux
Dr A Mijovic
Dr D Rees

Dr S Height
Dr M Awogbade
Dr A Ho
Dr R Patel
Dr S Schey
Dr R M Ireland
Dr R Marcus
Dr D Elebute

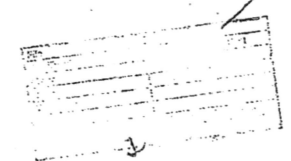

Dr Cathy Williams
Consultant Haematologist
Norringham City Hospital
Hucknall Road
Nottingham
NG5 1PB

Dear Dr Williams

Diagnosis: Relapsed myeloma
Withdraw from CRD trial after 9 cycles of combination chemotherapy
Bone marrow recovering
In complete remission

I reviewed Mavis in clinic today with her daughter and she is gradually recovering from pancytopenia induced by CRD. Her platelet counts have improved to 56 and her haemoglobin is stable at 10.4.

She remains in complete remission. She is having weekly G-CSF at the present moment and I suggested that she has G-CSF every Tuesday and has fortnightly blood tests on Mondays to see what her nadir neutrophil count is and we can decide whether we could stop the G-CSF or make it more infrequent.

I have asked her to keep off the Bonefos which she has now had for 5 years and she has mentioned some pain in her left shoulder and I suggested that she has an x-ray done from her GP surgery.

Her next review will be in 6-7 weeks time.   (Xray + shoulder
By Klare

Yours sincerely,

Dr Karthik Ramasamy
SpR in Haematology

SAGE on Bonefos
19 JAN 2009

BLOOD TEST (11·5-14·8) (4·5-13) (140-400) (2·0-7·5)
RESULTS   HB   WBC   PLATELETS   NEUTROPHILS   PARAPROTEINS
24 JAN 2011   13·1   5·8   162   2·7   9
31 JAN 2011 ------ TREATMENT BEGINS :-
26 FEB 2011   13·2   5·63   153   2·21   6
26 FEB 2011   12·4   4·73   113   1·61

9 AM — MAVIS MARY KNOTT
31st JANUARY 2011 BEGINS

Revlimid and Dexamethasone Drug Chart: (PARAPROTEINS 9)

31 JANUARY 2011
(DIAGNOSIS 22 FEB 2003)
(REVLIMID TRIAL 7 NOV 2007)

Day:	MON	TUES																										
Start Date: All Cycles	1	2	3	4	5	6	7	8	9	10	11	12	13	14	15	16	17	18	19	20	21	22	23	24	25	26	27	28
Lenalidomide Dose: 25mg		AT NIGHT ────																										
Dexamethasone Dose: 20 TABS 2mg		▓						▓							▓					▓		▓					
Other drugs:																												
Lansoprazole 30mg		ONLY																										
Aspirin 75mg		ONLY																										
Ciprofloxacin TWICE A DAY																												

BEFORE B/FAST— AM ──── (REDUCE ACID IN STOMACH) — BEFORE BREAKFAST
WITH AFTER FOOD — AFTER BREAKFAST →
CANCELLED 4·2·11 (DUE TO ALLERGY)

9 AM (WITH BREAKFAST)

20 (10 BREAKFAST / 10 WITH LUNCH WITH TEA) (WITH PORRIDGE)
9 AM BREAKFAST

※ DEXAMETHAZONE — TUESDAY
LANSOPRAZOLE (BEFORE FOOD)
ASPRIN AFTER or WITH FOOD)
(TWO HOUR GAP)

10³⁰ AM — {
BONOFOS — (NO MILK) 10³⁰ am
(MULTI VITAMINS 6pm) — WITH FOOD)
6 PM {
REVLIM (1) AT NIGHT
10³⁰ PM
10 BEDTIME
BONOFOS — (NO MILK)
(TO BE TAKEN WITH BONOFOS)

BONOFOS 800mg x 2
10³⁰ 10 AM 10³⁰ PM

(PLUS PRUNES / ALLBRAN & 2/3 LITRES FLUID) !

RESULTS CHART

Date	H B	WBC	platelets	neutrophils	paraproteins
16 8 10	13.1	4.91	111	2.86	5
25 10 10	13.1	4.71	123	2.49	7
8 11 10	12.7	5.4	116	2.2	8
13 12 10	13	5.17	136	2.4	7
24 1 11	13.1	5.8	162	2.7	9

REVLIMID & DEXAMETHAZONE TREATMENT begins 31 January 2011

	Date	H B	WBC	platelets	neutrophils	paraproteins
(1)	31 1 11	Revlimid treatment 25mg Dexamethazone 40mg				
(2)	28 2 11	13.2	5.63	153	2.21	6
(3)	28 3 11	12.4	4.73	113	1.61	4
(4)	18 4 11	12.4	4.59	98	1.16	3

(Steroids reduced to 20mg (10 tabs) - tough reduction)

(5)	23 5 11	12.7	4.38	88	1.13	2

(tolerated better – Thursdays still worst day)

(6)	20 6 11	12.5	3.33	95	0.81	2
(7)	18 7 11	12.6	3.86	84	1.00	2

(Dexomethazone halved to 10mg [5 tabs])

(8)	15 8 11	12.9	3.7	81	1.00	3

(Dr Williams reduced Revlimid to 15mg [from25mg])

(9)	12 9 11	12.5	3.10	75	0.73	3

Ninth month OFF ALL MEDICATION

	26 9 11	12.7	4.26	96	1.63	
(10)	10 10 11	12.6	3.89	87	1.5	3

(Revlimid 15mg now to be taken every other day. Steroids 10mg weekly)

(11)	7 11 11	13.2	4.73	118	1.75	4

(WELL - ENERGY HAS RETURNED!)

		HB	WBC	Platelets	Neutrophils	Paraproteins
		(11.5-14.8)	(4.5-13)	(140-400)	(2-7.5)	
(12)	5 12 11	13.1	5.07	133	1.66	4

STEROIDS 10mg NOW TAKEN DAYS 1 to 4 *(as Clinical Trial)*

(Wed)	28 12 11	13.0	4.96	113	1.25	5

(Kidney and calcium levels good) Revlimid raised to 10mg daily for 21 days of 28 day cycle
Dexamethazone 10mg days 1-4

(14)	30 1 12	12.9	4.66	138	1.36	6
(15)	27 02 12	12.9	4.64	107	<u>0.76</u>	**PP5!!**
(16)	26 03 12	12.9	4.23	106	<u>0.62</u>	5

(Remain on 10mg Revlimid & 10mg Dexamethazone days 1 to 4 after week off)

(Went home with GCSF and back again next week for blood tests - RESTED!)

	2 04 12	13.4	4.45	115	1.57	

BACK ON TRACK?

(17)	23 4 12	13 2	3.80	104	0.67	5

(GCS-F x 2 weekly begins today 23 April 2012)

(18)	28 5 12	12.3	4.92	130	1.69	5

(<u>Dexomethazone x 8mg tablets begin.</u> 2 - 8mg tablets days 1-4 with food breakfast & teatime)

(19)	25 6 12	12.3	6.58	140	3.43	5
(20)	23 7 12	13.2	4.05	123	1.28	5
(21)	28 8 12	12.5	6.5	116	2.6	5
(22)	19 9 12	12.9	7.19	119	3.79	5
(23)	15 10 12	12.6	4.46	126	1.60	5
(24)	12 11 12	12.9	5.97	121	2.51	5
(27)	4 Feb 13	12.6	5.99	108	3.04	5

!!'STABLE'!! *(GCS-F [Nivestim] reduced to 1 weekly confirmed)*

Session	date	HB	WBC	platelets	neutrophils	p proteins
(28)	22 3 13	12.9	4.36	135	1.35	6

(Dr Williams thought about upping Revlimid to 15mg – as appointment was a week early but decided to wait for paraprotein results. They were down to 5!)

(29)	29 4 13	129	12.27	114	8.79	5

(Took GCS-F last night as I forgot to take it on Thursday with above results!)

(30)	20 5 13	127	4.73	93	1.19	5

(Revlimid 10mg. Dexamethazone 8mg days 1–4 (2:2, 2:1, 2:2, 2:1) as discussed

(31)	24 6 13	129	5.74	122	2.89	4

(paraproteins not taken 24 6 13 so tested at Horncastle Medical Group)

(32)	22 7 13	129	5.74	122	4.1	6

(We have lots happening {MOVING!}. Dr Williams kindly suggested a month off steroids I hesitated then went for it. Did not ring for results. It was marvellous, felt so fit and well)

(33)	19 8 13	127	6.24	118	2.88	7

*(Revlimid 10mg. Dexamethazone days 1 – 4. 4 **8mg** tabs daily with breakfast(2) and teatime(2)*

(34)	16 9 13	125	12.16	111	8.55	6

(had taken GCS-F late (Sat) so unfortunately skewed results)

Dr Williams put Revlimid up to 15mg as paraproteins up to 7. But when I rang in on Thursday paraproteins had already come down to 6

(Realize having printed up the above diary details, I should have stuck with Dexamethazone 8mg x 4 tablets) Steroids are a tough challenge in the key to success.......

(47)	22 9 14	115	4.80	132	2.01	5

STABLE (week off)

(57)	13 7 15	120	6.20	131	3.17	6
(59)	7 9 15	125	6.8	130	3.6	6
(61)	20 11 15	124	6.39	123	2.76	6

Revlimid reduced to 15mg alternate days. Much better (11 tablets each session)

Dexomethazone 4 x 8mg days 1-4. Asprin 75mg. Bonefos 800mg x 2 daily. Nivestim injection weekly.

(62)	21 12 15	122	7.7	126	3.6	6
(70)	15 8 16	136	6.8	141	3.30	**STABLE**

		HB (11.5 - 14.8)	WBC (4.5 - 13)	Platelets (140 - 400)	Neutrophils (2 - 7.5)	Pproteins
(85)	18 9 17	137	12.24	143	8.89	7

(GCSF taken late Friday instead of Thursday)

(87)	20 11 17	136	5.99	166	2.49	7
(89)	15 1 18	136	6.54	166	2.47	8
(91)	12 3 18	133	6.10	182	5.57	9

(Pp 9 after severe cold/flu two weeks inside rest and recover. No normal busy exercise)

	9 4 18	134	6.83	162	3.86	8

9 April 2018   **REVLIMID TREATMENT STOPPED**

(Revlimid Treatment began 31 January 2011)

(Myeloma diagnosis Feb 2003)

DARATUMUMAB STUDY - *Need month clear of treatment before Study can begin*

9 May 2018 *Signed Study protocol.* Assessments begin. Bloods, bone marrow, x-rays, Pet Scan ....

9 July 2018		131	5.04	137	2.29	9

Study cancelled. *Paraproteins remain at* **9** (7 at Study centre) after *second* month re-screening. *Did not fit protocol.* Require Paraproteins 10 to begin Study. *Daratumumab Global Clinical Study assessment results.* Amazed to be told Myeloma is not active. *Immune system has adjusted itself. Carry on doing whatever you are doing! If we knew why we could find a cure.* **Pomalidomide** **when paraproteins rise.** (From July 2018 only Bonefos 800mg x 2, magnesium 250mg and multivitamins and minerals taken daily)

2 August 2018		132	6.31	139	3.02	10

Back to Overy Boathouse 15 September for some seafood, walking and wildlife

1 October 2018		135	6.12	153	2.94	9

!!Astonished. Results after five months *off* treatment!!

12 November 2018		136	6.14	153	2.75	9
17 December 2018		130	5.87	140	3.45	9
2 September 2019		135	5.25	139	2.55	10

REVLIMID *now approved for use in treating newly diagnosed patients, and patients at first relapse and for maintenance after autologous stem cell transplant*

WITH NORFOLK TERRIERS - SALTHOUSE BEACH.
Car park now taken over by grand undulating banks of shingle and stone.
Natural coastal processes are allowed. Opportunities for research. But the fishermen are still there.

THE AUTHOR

Since being diagnosed with Myeloma I have kept a diary. It helps enormously with treatment and it is easy to refer to reaction to drugs and dose and side effects. I eventually achieved my present 'stable' regime after nine years! Had hoped to reach it after the Revlimid Trial at Kings where amazingly, complete remission was achieved.

I grew up with a pony and a pair of roller skates, brownies, Sunday school, music lessons, choir practise, grammar school and on family caravan holidays, worked for my father in his building business and on the farm, qualified as a riding instructor, worked on a hunting yard in Leicestershire, took business studies and nursed sick children. It was the time of Nightingale wards when beds went into the middle for thorough cleaning daily. Sister took the food trolley round so she knew exactly what went in and the chart on the end of the bed recorded what went out! Matron did a daily round. It would have been an absolute sin to sit on a bed. We worked eight hours on four off with slight variations. Had to be in by 10pm or apply for a special late pass and could not request time off. When our long serving night sister asked the young doctor on duty 'How's your Bed State?' and he replied 'Mine's fine thank you, how's yours?' we couldn't believe our ears! We were paid £10 a month living in. Training school at St George's was inspiring. Matron Powell said 'Remember all you have learned here retain it and use it one day'. We had great nurses from abroad and from other hospitals coming in to train with us.

Having raised a family of our own, spending time with Pony Club, NHS non executive, riding young horses, studied horticulture; walking, gardening, writing, photography, home and family and enjoying the countryside with pony and trap and Norfolk terriers now keep us very busy.

As Matron Powell said 'Remember all you have learned here and use it one day'

'QUOTES' AND 'SAYINGS'
COLLECTED FOR INSPIRATION

Repair quarrels with laughter.

Friendship is God's most perfect gift

We have a duty to hope

Whatever one does one is

CALM. Take a minute. Take five breaths and listen to your own breathing. Think of nothing and tap into your reserves of calm.

Beautiful food is like beautiful music - a symbol of love

Stillness - that sense of peace - tranquility - a garden

Where the garden ends Fairyland begins

Be happy, be lucky and stay true to yourself

Don't be sad it eats into your soul.

A winning mindset

Be a good listener.

2500 year old Buddhist repeat meditation
'May I be filled with loving kindness
May I be well
May I be peaceful and at ease
May I be happy

A smile may make all the difference

The human mind that sometimes presumes to believes there is no such thing as a miracle is itself a miracle

Never miss the moment

With the right attitude you can achieve miracles

To love Life is to love God - Tolstoy

As the garden so the gardener

Happiness is a conscious decision. A commitment we make to ourselves

Chemotherapy is a tough expedition   Joc Forcyth

Simplicity. Patience. Compassion. These are your greatest treasures

If your heart is pure then all things in life are pure

A painting is the spirit of a human being in relationship to a sense of place

Live right, love well and do good

Simplicity is the way we open to everyday wonder

In each loss there is a gain and in every gain there is a loss and with each ending comes a new beginning

Nothing good is truly lost

TREATMENT 2003 to 2019

11 February 2003	*Diagnosis. Lincoln County. Paraproteins over **80**. Chemotherapy begins.* **THALIDAMIDE/CYCLOPHOSPHMIDE/DEXAMETHAZONE** *Drs Adelman, Pragnell and Speed.*
20 February 2003	*To Leicester. Change plasma. Blood transfusion Lincoln.*
17 March 2993	*Back in hospital on drip - couldn't eat, drink, take tablets.*
28-2 April 2003	*Admitted as the world spun round and round. Tried to write down what was happening - couldn't even write!*
4 April 2003	*Thalidamide/Allipurinol only. Blood transfusion*
22 April 2003	*Proteins 17 - continue Thalidamide only 200mg*
30 May 2003	*Thalidamide down to 100mg*
28 October 2003	*Thalidamide 75mg.* **Pararoteins down to 8.7** *(started over 80)*
Dec/Jan 2004	*Tried lower dose 50/25mg but could not continue due to peripheral neuropathy*
31 January 2004	*Robert and Elisabeth's Wedding*
October 2004	**STEM CELL TREATMENT** *Professor Russell* **Nottingham** *Proteins down to 5*
November 2005	*Shingles and chicken pox. Week of intravenous Aciclovir. Lincoln County.*
September 2006	**VELCADE TRIAL Nottingham.** *Proteins reduced to 23, 11, 8 and down to 6 with addition of Dexamethazone for last three sessions. Consultant Dr Cath Williams.*
7 November 2007	**REVLIMID TRIAL Kings, Denmark Hill, London.** *Consultant Dr Steve Skye Revlimid/ Cyclophosphomide/Dexamethazone* **<u>Complete Remission</u>**

REVLIMID MADE AVAILABLE ON NHS 2009

31 January 2011	**REVLIMID TREATMENT Nottingham** *Revlimid/Dexamethazone Dr Williams*
21 May 2016	**Westfield Gardens Open for National Gardens Scheme** *with tea and cakes to promote* **AWARENESS** *of Myeloma. A wonderful day. We welcomed over 200 visitors and raised £1,303.76p for MUK. Many thanks.*
10 Sept 2017	*Great North Run. Granddaughter Eliza raised £1,700 for Myeloma UK.*
9 April 2018	**REVLIMID TREATMENT STOPPED** *Session 92 (over seven years)*
2019	**OFF TREATMENT - STABLE - Results page 94**
29 July 2019	*SPEAKER. East Midlands Myeloma UK patients and family and friends Infoday and shared some favourite photographs.*

MAY
'and butterflies and breezes roam'

NOTES

NOTES

Printed in Great Britain
by Amazon